Planning
a Covid
Wedding

Insider Bride Guide

By

Lauren Jensen

Indie Publishing, LLC

ISBN: 978-1-7361005-2-3 (Paperback)
ISBN: 978-1-7361005-3-0 (e-book)
Library of Congress upon request.

Any references to historical events, real people, or real places are used fictitiously. Names, characters, and places are products of the author's imagination.

Front cover image by Aranprime
Unsplash.com/@aranprime

Back cover bio image by Marina Koslow
MarinaKoslowPhotography.com

Book design by Indie Publishing.
Cover design by Devin Jensen

Printed by Amazon in the United States of America.
First printing edition 2020.
Indie Publishing, LLC
942 Windemere Drive NW
Salem, OR 97304
www.insiderbride.com

Dedication

I dedicate this to all brides and grooms who need a sense of hope and stability during these turbulent times.

"When we love, we always strive to become better than we are. When we strive to become better than we are, everything around us becomes better too." - Paulo Coelho

Table of Contents

Introduction

Congratulations on your engagement, I'm thrilled to help you plan the wedding of your dreams! Even though we are living through a pandemic, we will all remember this time for better or worse.

In this workbook, I'll highlight all the areas to focus on for a flawless and memorable event. Since, Covid might be around for a while, this book will focus on things to devote your attention to while planning. Covid has taken over the event industry and caused a tremendous amount of angst for everyone involved. Many new state standards are mandated to make sure events are safe to the public. Every county is taking a different approach. Covid has impacted everyone differently this last year, and it has changed how we see the world we live in. Wedding planning will need to be flexible to paddle through these stormy waters. Covid regulations have also enormously affected travel. The travel industry has made many adjustments and taken a higher level of safety precautions. Lodging and hotels are making modifications to keep their customers safe. Entering into contracts during this time will involve a higher level of scrutiny to make sure you are legally protected. These are only the tip of the Covid iceberg that you will encounter during this bizarre time. I'll help you understand what is important for every different aspect of your events.

It might be nice for you to know a little bit about my background as a wedding planner. I grew up in the hospitality industry. My parents owned a restaurant and catering company that did weddings and large events. I always said events run in my blood because on-the-spot decisions come easy to me. My last position was at a luxurious, exclusive resort located in the high desert of Central Oregon with views of the Cascade mountain range surrounded by two golf courses. I was there for four years managing the special events, which included weddings and corporate retreats. I spoke in-depth to every bride, groom, mother, father, and maid of honor. We talked about every detail to make sure their wedding proceeded without a hitch. What I learned was that every event is unique and has its own special moments. I'm here to help you create the memories that you will cherish forever. Three years ago, I got married myself. I have a perspective of both the bride and an insider from the hospitality industry. We will navigate everything from flowers to your honeymoon. Let me share some of my best time and money-saving tricks of the trade with you.

This workbook will go through all of the possible agenda items for a wedding. It's your responsibility to narrow those down and decide what is truly important to you and your significant other. Feel free to write and add any ideas here. Use the Index as a way to choose your specific category. If you decide that a small or extra large wedding is more your style, don't worry. This workbook will still walk you through every detail you need. It's most important to keep this as simple as possible. This time of planning will be the happiest and most hectic. As a Covid bride, you will have more ups and downs than you'll expect to have. Buckle your seat belts and prepare for the emotional roller coaster we call planning a pandemic wedding.

"You know you're in love when you can't fall asleep because reality is finally better than your dreams."
- Dr. Seuss

Notes

Chapter One

Time for a plan!

L et's decide if you are having a small or large wedding. It comes down to the number of guests that will attend the ceremony and reception. My advice is to keep your wedding as simple as possible. This will save you many headaches. If you decide at any point to elope this book will go through all the same items you need to elope. The reason you might like the idea of an elopement versus a full wedding is the amount of work that needs to be done. Well, I'm here to tell you that might not be the case. An elopement can be just as elaborate as a large wedding with 100 guests. This will depend on you and your budget.

We are living through a pandemic, and this means we need to play it safe. Covid has taught us to stay home and limit the number of people we are in contact with daily. This could mean some of your guests are worried about traveling and won't be able to make an exception for your big day. Having an alternative virtual ceremony might be the answer for everyone. Talking to your family and close friends now will save you time and energy in the long run. Earnestly assess their willingness to attend in person or virtually. This comes down to saving lives. You don't want to remember your wedding day as anything other than amazing.

We can start by making your guest list. Fill out the section below with the most important people you want to invite. Keep adding people until you are ready to draw a line in the sand. Keep in mind your witnesses can be your parents, and your officiant could be a family member. Either way, with Covid rules they will be a part of the final number in your group at the ceremony. You can write names or guess the numbers in each line.

Bride & Groom:

Officiant:

Witness 1:

Witness 2:

Parents:

Step-Parents:

Grandparents:

Siblings:

Aunts:

Uncles:

Cousins:

Maid of Honor:

Bridesmaids:

Best Man:

Groomsmen:

Flower girls:

Ring Bearer:

Friends:

Co-workers:

Others:

At this point, you have the size of your wedding ceremony identified. With Covid it might be preferable to have a small ceremony now and a large reception later. Another choice is that you could do a small ceremony and reception now with an anniversary party down the road as your big reception. This is your decision and depends on how your family functions. There might be a lot of people left out of the list above. I have seen brides prioritize guest lists as the A group, the B group, and the C group. This allows you to invite more guests as the pending state-required event sizes are increased.

❑ Take the time to write down everyone you would invite if you could have a large wedding:

Before you reach out to any wedding vendors, let's talk about your budget. Ask the hard question upfront to be able to plan accordingly: who is paying for what? Traditionally, the bride's family pays for everything except for the rehearsal dinner. It's not that straightforward anymore. Families are currently splitting the costs into all types of ways:

- All sets of parents can help

- Bride & groom can round up some cash

- Grandparents or other family members can chip in

- Sometimes guests will offer to pay for a vendor as a wedding gift

- Credit cards can be used, but most vendors use cash, checks, or Venmo

Once you know your budget, you can start to break down the expenses. Below is a list of vendors and their average rates. Note that prices will vary depending on your location and season. These are very rough numbers. To get quotes specific to your area, you will need to reach out to the respective parties. These estimates can also vary depending on the number of guests. See more details on booking the vendors in Chapter 4. The low price means you are doing it yourself. This is why DIY is not always the best choice. Covid didn't make any of these prices go down. If anything, this pandemic has made all the numbers go up for the inconvenience of new state regulations and supplies needed to stay safe and clean. TheKnot.com has the most up-to-date numbers.

"Where there is love there is life."
- Mahatma Gandhi

Professional Range:	Wedding Average Costs:
Cake: $125 - $1,000+	U.S. average cost is $350
Catering: $1,800 - $20,000+	$40/per guest
Bar: $1,800 - $10,000+	$15-$40/per person pending type of alcohol
Décor: $300 - $5,000+	Depends on the type of décor
DJ: $600 - $5,000+	U.S. average cost is $1,000
Dress: $500 - $5,000+	U.S. average cost is $1,700
Dress Seamstress: $75 - $300	U.S. average cost is $150
Florist: $700 - $5,000+	U.S. average cost is $1,500
Hair: $150 - $600+	U.S. average cost is $150
Makeup: $150 - $600+	U.S. average cost is $150
Musicians: $200 - $5,000+	Depends on the number of musicians
Officiant: $250 - $800+	U.S. average cost is $300
Photographer: $1,500 - $10,000+	U.S. average cost is $2,000
Transportation: $150 - $10,000+	U.S. average cost is $800
Wedding Planner: $3,000 - $12,000+	U.S. average cost is $3,000
Wedding Day-of Coordinators: $1,250 - $3,000	U.S. average cost is $1,500

We need to start gathering the information into one place. Do you like Excel as much as I do? Google Sheets are a great way to have all your info no matter where you go. If you want to get a budget notebook, that's entirely your choice. Make sure you decide to use a familiar tool. This is not the time to learn QuickBooks to record your wedding expenses. Check out my personal wedding Google Sheet on the blog page of InsiderBride.com to start your template. The sooner you start this, the better. You will use this for every quote you get and payment you make. This will also have your to-do list and the guest list with their physical and email addresses.

Storytime

The first time I coordinated a wedding, was for a great friend of mine from Seattle. She was one of the most organized brides I've seen to this day. All she needed from me was to be the day-of coordinator. I thought this was an excellent plan and had no idea what I was getting myself into. Also, I did zero research. I just showed up. The bride handed me a list of items I needed to accomplish throughout the day. After I completed them, I could sit back, relax, and enjoy the rest of the night. There were a few hiccups that I saw that I'm not sure anyone else noticed. First, we were about to start the church ceremony, and it looked half full to me. I went to the bride to see if she wanted to stall and wait for a few more people to arrive. We ended up waiting 15 minutes, which doesn't sound like a long time, but when you're keeping a wedding schedule, that was an excruciatingly long wait. The ceremony began even though a few people showed up and snuck in the back. I made sure to call the catering company to say we were running 15 minutes late. They were not happy, but they understood these things happen at weddings. Next, the guests started to head down to the reception hall, which was a little spot on Lower Queen Anne. The Seattle Center was bustling with the Folklife Festival, an annual Memorial Day weekend celebration. This just so happened to be down the road from their reception hall. Which means there was no street parking at all. The guests circled for 20 minutes before they settled on the only parking lot left because it was terribly expensive. It was now time for the wedding party to line up for their announcement. We had collected almost everyone except one

9

groomsman who was parking his car. So, we waited and then waited a little longer and then we couldn't wait anymore. The group was heading into the hall and one of the bridesmaids was prepped and ready to walk in alone. Right as it was her turn to go in, he rounded the corner running at full speed. They were able to walk in together and no one in the crowd had any clue! The rest of the night went smoothly. I had pulled off my first wedding! I got a taste of the excitement, and the seed was forever planted all those years ago.

What is one piece of advice for couples?
"Plan a wedding that's unique to you as a couple. If you love going out for pizza, then consider having pizza as a late-night bite. It's those small touches that will help your guests truly enjoy your wedding. For planning during a pandemic, know that you can still have an amazing wedding that encompasses you as a couple, even if it's different from your original plan." - Brittney Gamble, Owner of Illuminate Your Night and Britt & Bixby Events

Notes

Chapter Two

Location,
location, location!

I t's time to look into your wedding location options. Do you already
have a concept in mind or several ideas? Are you thinking about a
destination wedding or a local affair? Do you dream about having
your celebration during your favorite season? Let's look at these choices a
little closer.

Hosting a wedding in the same town you live in is the easiest approach. It
makes scheduling all the appointments with vendors spread out over
time instead of all in one or two weekends. Most brides are worried
about booking things sight unseen, and I can agree with that. Everything
on a website looks better because they choose their best photos. Meeting
a vendor for lunch, coffee, or a drink after work is well worth it. Another
factor is all the items you'll bring to your wedding will start to add up.
The second most accessible location would be a place that is within an
hour from your home. Things change quickly in these Covid times, and
having the ability to find a new vendor the day before your wedding can
be easier if you know the town and can improvise. Choosing a place near
family members or parents is beneficial because you can directly send
boxes or Etsy.com items to them. They can also hold everything for you
if you jet off to your honeymoon right away. This person will already

need to be a part of your inner circle. You will begin to rely on them for more than you can imagine.

When picking a destination wedding, think about why you want to do this. Is it a special location or somewhere you have always dreamed about going? Maybe the venue is all-inclusive for weddings, which would be nice. Just remember that you'll need to travel there at least once for a destination wedding, but three to four trips are more reasonable. In January and February, most large cities host a wedding show with all the vendors. If you see a show scheduled, then plan that as one of your trips. Doing site tours at venues takes time, at least an hour or more at each place. Covid has changed our world to enable us to do almost everything online. More venues and vendors are meeting their potential couples on a video call. You can always ask if they will do a virtual site tour.

Choosing your favorite season could be the way you narrow down the place and month. There are two seasons in wedding land: in-season and off-season. This will vary depending on the location for winter vs. summer months. There could also be places that are summer year-round and don't have an off-season. When you are looking at venue pricing, it's always good to ask what is considered off-season. These prices can be up to half off or more for the site fee in the winter months. If you like the fall leaves, find out when they turn in that location, and then you'll have your month narrowed down.

"You don't love someone because they're perfect, you love them in spite of the fact that they're not." - Jodi Picoult

You're ready to start selecting your venue. There are many sites online to narrow down the choices: WeddingWire.com, TheKnot.com, etc. Before you make any calls, answer these questions:

❑ Do you want to have the ceremony and the reception in the same place?

❑ Do you also want to stay on-site where the reception is held?

❑ Do you want three different settings for the ceremony, reception and a place for your guests to stay?

❑ What type of beautiful backdrop are you looking for? Is it mountain views or ocean waves and sand in your toes?

❑ Do you have a month or season to focus on?

❑ What year do you plan to get married?

❑ How many guests do you imagine will attend?

It's good to have some ideas of what you want before making the calls. They will ask you many questions, write them all down to prepare to answer them for the next call.

Here are a few questions to ask the wedding sales department:

- Do you have any open dates in your time frame?
- If not, what do you have available for dates?
- Do you have an online wedding brochure with menus you can email?
- What is your site fee for weddings?
- When is your off-season?
- Do you have a Food & Beverage Minimum?
- What is your standard gratuity or service charges?
- Do you have room block requirements?
- What changes have you made for Covid?
- Have your sanitation standards changed?
- What are your state-mandated event restrictions right now?
- What phase are you in?
- What needs to happen for your state to get to the next phase?
- Have your Covid cases been going up or down in the past month?
- When can you do a site tour?
- Have you done virtual site tours?

Site tours are a great way to see everything in person. Take pictures of any of the banquet rooms you plan to hold events. Check out all the different event spaces to see all of your options. If they have hotel rooms available to look at, take a peek! It is good to call ahead and set a time to do this. If you drop in and check out a place without calling, you might not get anyone available to do a tour. If you call ahead, the sales team will be ready for your visit. Check out the banquet menu and the regular restaurant menu while you are there. If you have time to have a quick appetizer or a meal, it will give you a better idea of the food they can produce. I would say you could pull off three site tours in a day, but that means you are taking great notes and pictures to retain all the information. Everything will start to blur together after a while.

A site fee is a very typical cost for a wedding. The majority of venues will charge a site fee to hold the wedding date. This is frequently a non-refundable payment. Some venues will charge only a site fee if they offer nothing else. It's important to know what comes with the site fee. There will be a list in the brochure, and if you don't see it, ask for it in the contract or an email. Many things can come with this fee: tables, reception chairs, linen, silverware, glassware, dance floor, bars, ceremony chairs, arch, etc. The more the site fee, the more will come included. Remember, anything they don't provide you will need to rent from somewhere else and bring in yourself.

It is a good idea to get a contract from at least two venues for comparison purposes. Yes, that does mean going through the whole process and then having to say no to someone. That's why emails were invented. When you are looking over your contract, make sure all the names are spelled correctly and the dates and times are accurate. What is noted wrong on the contract will be very costly to change later. Ask someone in your family to read it over with you. In this time of Covid, you need to look for a paragraph called "Force Majeure." If it's not in your contract, ask for it to be added. This is the only thing saving current weddings from losses. It basically says if any unforeseen circumstances are preventing your wedding from happening, the contract is void. Most couples in March of 2020 decided to move their wedding to later in 2020 or into 2021. If you are looking at 2021 dates, you might find that 2021 is full already. You'll be pushed into 2022. This means 2022 is filling up quickly. The sooner you set the date, the better.

The venues should be well versed in the Covid restrictions that apply to their location. So, ask them! Find out what they are doing to keep everyone safe. Look at their new policies on sanitation and employee wellness. If they are not knowledgeable on the Covid restrictions, that is a red flag. You can look for overall cleanliness on your tour. It's good to know if you're responsible for providing hand sanitizer or other disinfectant products. Are you required to have a sanitation station with gloves and masks? Are you able to mark the 6-foot lines on the floor in places you'll have bar lines, or will they do that for you? Will there be extra staff wiping surfaces, or do you need to provide people for that? Will there need to be a bathroom attendant to clean during the event? Basically, find out what your responsibility is and what they will provide for your events.

When you book a venue with guest rooms, there could be a need for a room block. This is a contract between you and the hotel saying you will fill a specific amount of rooms by a certain date. The minimum number of rooms is usually 10. The cut-off date falls between 30 and 90 days before your weekend. These are the benefits for you to block off rooms:

- All of your guests can stay in one place

- There will be fewer transportation costs and logistics

- Fewer people getting lost or being late for the events

- Room rates are lower with group rates

It is good to have an idea of how many rooms you will need for your wedding. This might be a short email to your guests asking if you got a room block would they be interested. You could also talk to the last person in your family who got married and ask what they did. It comes down to two days: the one before the ceremony and the actual ceremony. Most guests will arrive the day before and want both nights, but not always. Your contract will need to say how many rooms you are holding onto each night. If you want to guess the number of rooms, that is not a problem because overestimating is a good thing! Knowing your cut-off date is the key. This is the last day you will be able to drop rooms that your guests have not booked. Your hotel will be able to provide you a list of all the guests who have already booked. Since every hotel is different, it is best to ask about your options before signing a room block contract.

What is a "food and beverage minimum" compared to a site fee? There could be both or just one, depending on the place you choose. If you go with a venue that offers on-site catering, this contract will have both fees. The Food and Beverage (F&B) minimum is the actual amount of food and beverages ordered on the day of the wedding. If you are planning to have a reception after your ceremony there will classically be a cocktail hour with appetizers, reception dinner, and an open bar. Think about how you would like your night to go after the ceremony:

❏ Is it a short night ending after dinner?

❏ Or do you want to go on dancing until midnight?

Wedding venues are charging on average $125/per guest for the F&B minimum. For example, if you have 100 guests at $125/per person, your F&B minimum would be $10,000. If you have 10 guests, your F&B minimum would be $1,250. The venue will still charge you for the full amount even if you don't spend the full amount on food or beverages. Don't forget the taxes, gratuity, or service charges on top of the F&B minimum. The math looks like this:

- 4 drinks on average with $10 average price per drink = $40/per person for drinks
- A meal for about $50/per person
- Appetizers for about $35/per person
- Give or take a few to make up the $125/per person

There are many ways to make sure you reach your desired minimum. Your on-site event planner should assist you with these numbers. You might need to ask for a breakdown if they don't share one with you. Your cost can be compiled after you have made your food choices. This is called your banquet check. Which is different from your Banquet Event Order (BEO). The BEO is a full outline of your entire day, including food, beverages, schedule, and any other details you have outlined with your internal event planner. If you don't see a detail on your BEO it could be forgotten. Make sure to read this document very carefully. This could make or break your wedding.

A cocktail hour will keep your guests entertained while you sign your wedding certificate and take a few photos after the ceremony. This means drinks and appetizers. Appetizers can go two different ways: passed by a server or at a buffet station. When you are ordering your appetizers, it's good to have a variety of red meat, chicken, seafood, or vegetarian items. Usually, four bites per person will keep everyone satisfied and won't be too much to spoil their dinner. If you choose three of the best appetizers, everyone will automatically try a new one but will only go back for a second bite of their favorite. If you know your group loves bacon-wrapped prawns, order enough for everyone to have two of each. If you are short on your F&B minimum, this is an excellent place to add 5 or 6 bites of food per person, so you never run out of appetizers. If you go with a buffet station of appetizers, there will already be a lot more because of how a buffet station works. For example, if you order a vegetable crudité platter and have 10 guests, the Chef will most likely prepare enough grilled asparagus for everyone a sufficient amount. Having food out for guests to help themselves can go both ways. Some guests will fill up a plate and go back for more. Some will not even see the table or find the time to go over and have a bite. The majority of the time, there will be food leftover at an appetizer station.

❏ What are your ideas about the appetizers?

Let's get into the booze! Here are some preliminary questions:

❑ Are you going to have a full bar?

❑ Wine and beer only?

❑ Whiskey and cigar bar?

❑ What is your favorite drink?

❑ Your partner's preferred cocktail?

❑ What do your parents like to drink?

❑ Will you allow shots?

There are so many choices and exploring Pinterest doesn't make it any easier. It usually comes down to who is paying for the bar bill. The bar is where you can spend massive amounts of money by accident. Most venues will let you build a bar from their packages. There are so many ways to do this, and it really comes down to your family traditions. Most east coast weddings have a hosted bar always and forever. A hosted bar means there is only one running tab and everyone else receives complimentary drinks, also known as an open bar. West coast weddings have started a new trend of a cash bar. A cash bar allows your guests to pay for their own drinks with cash or a card. I've seen a combination of both a cash bar and a hosted one work well. Here are some scenarios:

First – Hosted cocktail hour with beer, wine, champagne, non-alcoholic and signature drinks. Wine service or bottles on the table for dinner and a cash bar for everything after dinner until the end of the night.

Second – Hosted beer, wine, champagne, and non-alcoholic drinks all night. Cash bar for liquor drinks all night.

Third – Hosted signature drinks all night, cash for the rest.

If you happen to be purchasing all the alcohol yourself and setting up a self-serve bar at your location, I can make suggestions. I said earlier 5 drinks is the average for a wedding guest from 5:00pm to midnight. Any shorter, you can start to cut back on the number of drinks per person. Even if a venue is doing this for you, it's good to know the details:

Beer keg: Everyone wants kegs! It just makes sense if your group can finish a keg. Pony kegs have 62 pints of beer, and full kegs have 124 pints of beer. Kegs are expensive upfront but pay off in the end. If you are charged $500 for a pony keg, the beers cost $8/each, and with a full keg, they cost $4/per beer. The type of beer you choose will decide the price. Most breweries and some grocery stores will sell you a keg without going through a vendor. You will also need to put down a keg deposit and get a tap handle. These will all need to be returned by someone in your group after the event. Don't forget to keep the keg chilled!

Bottled beer: With a small group, it's easier to get a few cases of beer. Think about the guests who will drink beer and what they like. Choose a beer the groom will like. It could be something local or his favorite beer. If you go with a heavy IPA, make sure you also get a light beer to go along with this. You can use the same formula as with the wine (see below) to figure out how many cases to buy. It's always good to have an extra case of beer. It can be taken to the next party on your wedding weekend. Consider a non-alcoholic beer if you have adults that would like this option.

Champagne: This is always good to have on hand. Most women like to drink a glass of champagne on special occasions. If that is your only target audience, 2-3 bottles should be fine. There is a chance you will have an impromptu champagne toast. If you want to do this, make sure you have the correct glasses and enough bottles for everyone. A bottle of champagne goes further than a wine bottle. You can serve 6-10 drinks from one bottle of bubbly. Plus, the glasses don't need to be completely full for a toast. For 10 guests, 2 bottles would be good, but remember that they will go back to the bar looking for more once you give someone champagne. Another fabulous idea is tray passed champagne upon the arrival of your guests. This is a nice touch to any size wedding!

Liquor & specialty drinks: Go back to your favorite drinks. If you don't drink liquor do you need it at your reception? Or if you hands-down drink a margarita on the daily, you should have them as your specialty drink! Specialty drinks are funny because they mean a lot to you, but someone else might say, "Oh, I can't handle tequila anymore!" You'll have a full batch that no one drinks. This is one thing I would skip altogether, but that's just me! To figure out what to serve in general, pick the basics: vodka, whiskey, and tequila. Or if you only prefer gin, add that to the mix. Another great combo is vodka, whiskey, and Bailey's. These make a variety of cocktails that even go well with coffee. When you buy liquor, it comes in a single bottle or a case. You can figure an average of every guest having two liquor drinks, and each bottle of 750ml serves around 16 drinks. It's really all right to shoot high when ordering since it's best not to run out, as long as you have the means to take it home later.

Non-alcoholic drinks: If you are in charge of getting these, find a place that will take back unopened cases. Then you can buy as much of anything you like. You'll need soda water, 7up, Coke/Pepsi, tonic water, OJ, and cranberry juice for a basic bar. You can pair that down further if you don't drink tonic. Make sure you are buying things you want to go home with later. The juices are good for kids at the reception. Iced Tea and Lemonade are a lovely touch if you're going to do a non-alcoholic drink station. A coffee station is always nice after dinner for a crowd that likes coffee. These are excellent additions but might not be allowed with the Covid rules.

Wine: Look at the season you are serving and choose a red and a white. If you are serving in the summer get more white wine and get lots of red in the winter. If you don't want to run out of wine and wouldn't mind having the extra go home with you: count an average of 4 glasses of wine per person. Here are the calculations:

- 20 people x 4 glasses = 80 glasses of wine / 4 glasses in each bottle = 20 bottles of wine.

There are 12 bottles in a case, so you could get a case of each and be good. Except if you plan to do wine for dinner. A wine service means someone will go around and pour a glass of wine while everyone is seated. Or you could set 2-3 bottles on each table. This will increase the wine by 1-2 glasses per person. They might not have opted to get up and get one from the bar, but now that it's right in front of them, how can they resist? If you are willing to run out of wine, lower the math to:

- 2 glasses of wine per person (20 people x 2 glasses = 40 glasses of wine / 4 glasses in each bottle = 10 bottles of wine).

There are corkage fees ranging from $15-$30/per bottle if you are going to a resort. Corkage fees are charged for any wine that you bring into the venue. It is not always the most cost-effective way unless the wine is free to you. If you bought a $10 bottle at the store and then paid $25 at the resort, your wine is $35/per bottle. Resorts will work with you to order wine off their wine list or do special orders.

Bar essentials: If you are in charge of setting up a self-serve bar, these are all the items you'll need:

- Bartenders are valuable in keeping your guests happy. I would recommend 1 bartender per 50 guests. If you have a self-serve bar, it's still important to put someone in charge of setting it up and breaking down. If this same person can keep an eye on the bar for refilling during the night, that's good with a lively crowd.

- Ice: it's always good to have more than you need. It will be for chilling the beer, wine, champagne, and soda. It will also be used to fill a glass with ice. Round up as many coolers as you can and have one for each type of alcohol. Find a nice bucket to go on top of the table for guests to scoop their own ice. It's nice to have 1-2 ice scoops.

- Water is a must. There are large beverage dispensers with a pour spout on the bottom. A few pitchers can also be helpful.

- Glassware is a difficult decision when you are trying to save the planet. Of course, plastic is easier, cheaper, and has less breakage. On the other hand real glass is super classy. It's almost impossible at a self-serve bar to do real glass because the bartender is usually the one to stock and clean each one for re-use. In these Covid times, reusing glasses is not sanitary, so using a new glass every time is the most hygienic way to go.

- A bar sign is a nice touch to let your guests know what is available. Even labeling the coolers is a small detail that won't go unnoticed.

- Garnish: lemons and limes are all you really need. If you have a small group of 10, you could get by with 2 of each cut in wedges. A larger group of 20 guests would need 5 of each pre-cut. If you are going above and beyond, you could add olives, cocktail onions, or maraschino cherries.

- Additional items: you'll need a few wine bottle openers. Salt and sugar can be used for the rim of a glass. Or sugar for iced tea and salt for tequila. Trash bins, cutting boards, knives, and bar towels are necessary. Cocktail napkins are a nice touch but not absolutely necessary. Wedding printed napkins for guests to easily take home are an excellent favor.

- Serving license: it's essential to check the state requirements for serving alcohol on private property. There can still be requirements for liquor licenses for the bartender or the property. Especially in a time of Covid it's crucial to follow requirements for sanitation.

"More smiling, less worrying. More compassion, less judgment. More blessed, less stressed. More love, less hate." - Roy T. Bennett

What are you excited about serving at your reception?

❑ Beer:

❑ Wine:

❑ Champagne:

❑ Liquor:

❑ Specialty drinks:

❑ Non-alcoholic drinks:

Storytime

It was an hour before the ceremony started, and we went out to make sure the ceremony chairs were perfect. We showed up just in time to see the arch blow over exactly where the bride and groom would have been standing. We started hustling around to see if we could get it upright. Luckily, we did, and my assistant stood holding the arch until I could return with a member of our maintenance team. They were able to secure it with a few boards. Then we staked it into the ground, as well as roped it down. We were able to pull this off without anyone in the wedding knowing it happened. From that point on, stakes were required for all arches, no matter what season it was or whether the wind was blowing or not.

Notes

Say yes to the dress!

W hat can you do during the endless wait for the date to get figured out? People say it takes a year to plan a wedding. I totally agree with this. There are many decisions to make, so rushing your special day is not a great idea. You will have a lot of downtimes, so look at the few categories below for my suggested activities.

Dress: All the ladies in your life are excited about your engagement, or they should be. Let's go shopping! Start with the dress shops in your own town. Book an appointment and take a few friends. Most dress shops are offering private sessions because of Covid. Some even let you bring in a bottle of champagne! It's good to have a few styles in mind. Wedding dresses are not like your typical dress. It takes a village to get you in and out of them. Remember to bring a white or nude strapless bra, wear underwear you don't mind people seeing and heels in the same height you plan to buy. What you have in mind in the beginning is not always what you end up with. Be open-minded. It might take a few dresses to find the right one. You'll know the minute you see it in the mirror. My dress criteria were no lace or beads. I wanted an effortless silk dress and mine turned out much different. Shops will have a variety of items that go with your dress like shoes, veil, jewelry, and purses. Before you buy your shoes, it's good to know where your ceremony will take place. If your ceremony takes place on grass or a sandy beach, then stiletto heels are not the way to go, unless you plan on using heel protectors.

It's good to know white is the color people will identify you as the bride for all your other parties. You don't have to wear white, but it does make sense. If you see a white dress while shopping that is not perfect for your wedding dress, buy it because it could be perfect for the bridal shower, rehearsal dinner, or your bachelorette. I bought a few white shirts as well, which worked out because our rehearsal dinner was in much colder weather than we expected in June.

Research: This is also a time to do research. Everything can take hours to figure out. When will you have time to do the research, and how will you start to compile all of your findings? Can you do everything online or order in magazines? You can go shopping at all the bridal stores in your town, or you can call friends and ask what they would do again at their weddings. It's a perfect time to get out there without having to make any hard decisions yet. Check Pinterest and Etsy for ideas. It's best to take screenshots of the items you like and add them to a Word Doc with sections for hair, makeup, décor, flowers, etc. You will use this later to show each vendor your wedding style. Like a vision board, it's an inspiration board for your wedding.

DIY: Will you be attempting any do-it-yourself items? This always seems easy and cost-effective in the beginning. In the end, it's more frustrating than it's worth. Don't DIY if you don't love crafting. Stick to what you're good at and always leave more time than you expect. Start the DIY items as soon as possible. I had a few items that looked easy to make, and after they turned out not even close to what I wanted, I scratched them.

Planning other parties! The planning never ends! You can always plan something. Here are some to choose from: engagement party, bachelorette, bachelor, and bridal shower. See Chapter 9 for more details on each party. Engagement parties aren't happening anymore in general. They have turned into small parties with friends, which is perfect for

Covid. Bridal showers occur closer to the wedding, so that gives you time to think about what you'd like to do. Bachelor and bachelorette parties are also getting canceled for Covid. Be careful what you decide to do and the timeframe. You could always look for local planners that have experience planning these types of parties, such as this company BendVacations.com. That's especially helpful if you don't live in the area, they will have the most current information. The further out you can push these parties, the better. Smaller is better, but that depends on your circle of friends.

❑ What are your initial ideas about these different parties?

_____

_____

_____

Paper: There will be a few items that are connected to the same design. These are the ones to start at: the invitations, envelopes, menus, signs, table numbers, escort cards, programs, thank you cards, postcards, and itineraries. You can begin research on local calligraphers that are focused on weddings. Some outside wedding planners can help you order these items. There are many websites where these documents can be done, and Minted.com is the most popular. They can even match your invitations to your wedding website. Start to make your website as soon as possible, then add your new info along the way. Escort cards are for the table with the person's name, menu choice, and table number. For more tips on escort cards, table numbers and reception seating go to the blog page on InsiderBride.com.

There are also the save the date, postponed, and uninvited cards. Covid has put most couples in a dilemma about what to do if the wedding was already planned. If you have already sent out the save the date cards and you are now downsizing, then the uninvited cards are the way to go. This will kindly let your guests know that the wedding has been downsized due to unforeseen circumstances. If you are rescheduling the date to next summer, then a postponement card will be the better choice. This card will let your guests know the new date and your website link for more information. The best way to approach these situations is to be honest and prompt. This courtesy lets guests know before they book anything non-refundable. Since they are your close family and friends, they will hear how you eventually got married, so it does make sense to be candid. Anyone who has been through the wedding planning process will understand. Depending on your list size it could be a phone call, email, personal written card, or generic card. If you can do a ceremony and live stream it, your guests could still be invited to the ceremony and not feel left out or obligated to travel. Your wedding planner will be very supportive during this task because all of their couples are going through the same thing. Your invitations go out about three months before. They include all the RSVP cards needed for that weekend. If you have rehearsal dinner or brunch, include those all on one card. On this card or the return envelope have a spot for their name. It sounds silly, but I received a few that didn't include the names! Ask about dietary restrictions along with their dinner choices. For Covid reasons, you can add a line asking whom they feel comfortable sitting with at dinner and if it's anyone outside of their household. Lastly, you can add driving directions and your website for the most updated information.

Wedding Party: Choosing your Bridesmaids and Groomsmen is expected pretty early. Your best friends will want to help planning because of all the time we have at home during Covid! There have been many different ways to tell them you have picked them as a part of your team. There are even specialty wine bottle labels you can make to ask your bridesmaids. Your wedding party will spend a lot of money to help you get married. In return, you are

Etsy Seller: Everbloomingevents

expected to give them a gift as a token of your appreciation. There are so many ideas of what to get for your wedding party. For the ladies, it's nice to pay for some or all their expenses. These could be shoes, dress, hair, or makeup. I've seen matching robes or special personalized cups. For the guys, the same idea applies. If you can help pay for any of their matching ties or rentals, that's always nice. Other gifts are a nice bottle of whiskey or a flask.

❑ How would you like to find out you were someone's favorite person?

❑ What gift ideas do you have in mind?

Gifts: You'll be getting lots of gifts over the next year from your registry. It's good to register as soon as possible because some family members like to send engagement gifts. You can get creative in places to register. Two or three places are normal: Target, Macy's, Crate & Barrel, Amazon, or even REI. If you want to accept cash for honeymoon funds instead of presents, check out Zola.com.

There are many presents you can give, as well. You can surprise your parents with a way to remember your wedding day. There are embroidered handkerchiefs or engraved jewelry on Etsy.com. For your siblings and wedding party, it can be something more fun! I have seen gifts go out to the vendors or anyone that helped with your planning. My aunt was a big part of setting up the décor, and I made sure to give her something special.

Last of all, are you considering sending gift bags to the hotel rooms? When you begin planning, this seems like a great idea, but it could change. These bags can be more than you're expecting to organize, and the price might be too high in the end. A lovely bag would include wine, snacks, local items, maps, or your itinerary. Once you get all the items purchased and packed, you will still need to organize them. Ask your hotel for a list of guests and arrival dates from your room block. Start to tag the bags with the exact name on the reservation. That is the only way the hotel will deliver the bag to the correct room. Make sure to assign someone to deliver the bags to your hotel before your first guests arrive. For more tips on gift bags go to the blog page on InsiderBride.com.

❑ What are your thoughts on gifts?

Favors: Are you giving out any favors? Should you purchase matching masks or have generic ones available? The number of guests attending will dictate the price you can spend on the favors. Right now, check out everything you would like to give your guests. I decided to keep it simple and provide a combination

Etsy Seller: Megmichelle

thank-you note and flower seeds. Most of my guests were traveling, so this worked perfectly. The small envelope cost about $1.50 each, and the flower seeds were $50. I liked the personalized thank you note on the back, and if people never planted the seeds, that was ok. Maybe ten years from now I'll go to a cousin's house, and they'll show me the flowers that bloom every year from our wedding.

❑ What are your ideas about the favors?

_____

_____

_____

Supplies: You will need a bag of supplies for setup and getting ready. This bag will save you over and over again. Make sure you have the following:

- Two pairs of scissors
- Box of assorted size band-aids
- Clear packaging tape
- Duct tape
- Handful of zip ties
- A small sewing kit
- Extra Sharpies
- Extension cords and phone chargers
- Wine bottle opener
- Tide stain remover stick
- A package of assorted size safety pins
- T-pins are great for hanging signs to chairs or walls that have fabric
- Two or four long lighters if you have candles to light
- Package of bobby pins
- A bride kit has more specific items

❏ Anything else you want to remember to bring:

_____

_____

_____

_____

Theme: Themes can be simple, modern, elegant, a rustic barn, or maybe you're having a Game of Thrones theme. It will either be what you genuinely like or how you've always envisioned your wedding. The venue will help you make this come to life. Don't buy décor until you have signed your contract with your venue, so you don't waste any money.

EtsySeller: ThePinkOwlDesigns

❏ What are your thoughts about a theme?

_____

_____

_____

_____

_____

Dancing: Do you love or despise it? Either way, you'll have to decide which dances you'd like to do or do without. If you have always wanted to take ballroom dancing lessons, this is the time to sign up. The earlier you sign up, the better you'll be. Once you have found your songs, try the dances with your groom to be, and your father. At the very least, talk about how the dance will go and if it involves any dips. It's never a good idea to try a surprise dip in a wedding dress.

The Kiss: Practice makes perfect, isn't that what they say? This will be a kiss in front of all your friends and family, something you might not have ever done. Let's break this down, shall we! Start filming with your phone and say, "You may now kiss the bride!" You should practice kissing for two full seconds and actually count. Now check to see if this looks natural. If it felt awkward, take a step back and do it again. What I have seen work well is the groom will put his arms around the bride's waist or rest on her hips. The bride will hold the shoulders or neck of the groom. Try to avoid holding each other's faces. That's never great for pictures. Speaking of photos, make sure someone tells your officiant to step to the side with the wedding party. If your officiant is a lady, they should step towards the bridesmaids, and for a male, they should join the groomsmen. This will give you a full shot of you kissing with an amazing background and not someone smiling at you.

"I heard what you said. I'm not the silly romantic you think. I don't want the heavens or the shooting stars. I don't want gemstones or gold. I have those things already. I want...a steady hand. A kind soul. I want to fall asleep, and wake, knowing my heart is safe. I want to love, and be loved."
- Shana Abe

Story Time

We were about to start the ceremony. The stage was set at the top of the grand staircase, the entrance to the wedding on the event lawn below. I was at the top of the stairs, and at the bottom was the outside coordinator directing traffic. My job was to send the wedding party down the stairs. First, the groom departed with his groomsmen in tow. Next went the godfather of the bride who was also her officiant. I left the bride's parents at the top of the stairs and told them to wait for me to come back. I turned around to go get the bride and bridesmaids in the clubhouse just 25 feet away. Before I could bring them out, I heard screaming. I told her to wait in the seats next to the fireplace, and I would see what happened. I came back to a frantic scene of people running all over. I looked down and saw the officiant had fallen and was lying on the cement landing. He looked up right before taking his last step and missed it. He went flying headfirst into a cement wall surrounding the stairs. I ran over to see what I could do, but all of the proper medical attention was being taken care of. I went back to the bride and closed the doors. I said in my calmest voice possible, "We need to stay here for a little bit longer. Does anyone need anything at this time?" I still give her so much credit because she stayed seated and calm without knowing what was going on at all. I called my boss, the Director of Sales & Marketing, and asked her to come to the clubhouse. She was staying onsite that weekend because she was also the Manager on Duty. She came running. All I remember saying to her was, "Man down," and I pointed in his direction. She could tell I was a frantic mess. I took off sprinting for something. She started running in circles like the rest of our F&B staff. Once we got the bleeding under control and a bandage wrapped around his head, we were able to talk to him. He said, "I'm still going to do the ceremony!" We all looked at each other and said, "No, that's not a good idea. You need to go to the hospital!" He said, "I will only go to the hospital after the ceremony." Three other ordained people in the crowd offered to do the ceremony. Meanwhile, the crowd watched all of this happen, and we were running about 15 minutes late. It was time to make a big decision. I had a conversation with the bride's parents and they said, "It doesn't make sense to have him do the ceremony, but ultimately it is up to the bride. She can make the final decision." We all went in together to let her know what happened and ask her a pretty big question. I was waiting on the outskirts of the conversation to let them talk it through. She decided if he feels this strongly, then she does want him to do the ceremony. Once we had that information, we let the officiant know he could only do the ceremony only if there was a car waiting to take him away after the ceremony and a wheelchair staged right behind him during the ceremony. He agreed to the terms. The music went back on, the groomsmen wheeled him down the aisle. The bridesmaids carefully made their way down. Our bride made it all the way to her wedding, and her godfather stood through the whole ceremony. One of our cars drove him straight to the emergency room with his wife. He got 11 stitches in his forehead, and sure enough, he made it back to the dance floor to have a dance with his goddaughter by 11:30 PM. This was not a wedding you'll ever forget!

What have you changed in your business to account for Covid?

"We have implemented extra steps to sanitize all rentals as they come back. We are being very careful when handling dirty dishes, added sanitization steps for them as well. We are all wearing masks while working and driving together. This has definitely added expenses, but I have chosen not to charge my clients anything extra."
~ Kimi Chassie, Owner of Curated Events

Notes

Chapter Four

It's time to pick
the wedding team!

Your location is booked and confirmed! This means you have a date and a place to tell the vendors. Looking into all the vendors is fun to do, but now you have an actual day to compare to their schedule. If you can have two to three narrowed down by this point, you can start reaching out and see what they have open. There is a fine line between saving your date and making a deposit to hold the date. Make sure that is clear with the person you are working with. If you book too soon, you can't change your mind, and if too late, your date will be gone. Do your research to make sure this company will still be operating in the next few years. With Covid everything can be a little frantic, but staying calm has always worked for me! There could be additional waivers to sign with vendors to slow the spread of the disease. There might even be additional handling steps to follow to keep you, your guests, and your vendors safe. It's best to ask each vendor what their policies are and that you both agree on the terms before signing a contract.

On their website, you'll get a vibe immediately, but it's their personality that counts. When you get along instantly with someone, you'll know this will be a great fit. Once you book your first vendor, ask them who they enjoy working with for your next few categories. Maybe they have a preferred vendor list they can share with you. Make sure you follow them on Instagram for inspiration along the way. Your vendors make all the difference and will give you incredible energy to start your big day!

Cake & Desserts: One of the reasons people love going to weddings is an excuse to eat cake! I have seen big, small, bold, classy, and comical cakes. The number of guests will dictate the size you need. Having the perfect cake topper could be the only reason you want a cake. It's exciting to go to a cake tasting and try all the different types. You can also consider other desserts like donuts, pies, macaroons, s'mores, or cupcakes. It's all up to you! Maybe you decide not to do a formal cake cutting, and a table full of candy is more your style. This comes down to your and your partner's favorite sweets. Answer the questions below on your preferences:

❑ What are your favorite types of cake?

❑ What are your partner's favorite types?

❑ What other desserts do you both like?

❑ If you didn't do something sweet, what would you do?

Catering: If you've chosen a resort with an onsite catering team or you need to find a catering company, there are a few things to keep in mind. There is still a lot to decide to matter who is preparing your food. When you book a resort, they will never let you bring in your own food. That's just a rule. Let's dive into the food.

For the plated meal, 90% of the guests will choose a steak, and the other 10% will be having the fish, chicken, or a vegetarian meal. I know you want to be creative in this aspect; almost every couple does. If your Chef makes an amazing filet mignon, go with it, don't question this choice at all. Your guests will be happy. Steak is one choice, and the other one is where you can finally be original. Go back to what you or your significant other actually like to eat. Is it fish, chicken, or pork? See what the menu has to offer that is a step above what you normally eat. When you do a plated meal, you have the option to pre-set your salads on the table before guests arrive. Plated meals always require someone to make the escort cards.

If you are going in the direction of a buffet, this makes sense for twenty guests or more. You will either build the buffet yourself, from the salad to the dessert or choose from a preset list. You can always add action stations, such as a roast beef carving table or an ice cream sundae station. A buffet is a great way to provide food for everyone if there is not a set time for dinner or want people to be able to go back for round two. The buffet can stay out for an hour or more. If you choose a plated dinner for the reception, then a buffet could be good for the rehearsal dinner. It has a more casual approach to serving a meal. A buffet doesn't require escort cards! All this being said about a buffet, you might not even have this option because of Covid. Self-serve stations were the first thing to go at every grocery store and restaurant. These are very hard to regulate and keep sanitary. A self-serve station can include a food buffet, desserts, appetizers, and even drink stations. Asking your catering team is always the best option. Maybe they could provide servers to handle the food or put up Plexiglas dividers.

A family-style meal is very popular right now. Think of it as a mix between a plated dinner and a buffet. The server will bring large platters and bowls directly to each of the tables. This will give your guests a chance to pass the dishes and make new connections. For your entrée items, I highly recommend serving the individual steak or salmon straight to the guest that requested it on their RSVP. This will alleviate someone not getting a salmon or steak of their choice. Another essential item to remember for a family-style meal is to have large tables. You need enough room for at least five or six large platters in the center of the table. A round table works perfect for this, as long as you don't add too many flowers or décor. Ask your catering manager if you are required to do escort cards for each person with your family-style meal.

Kid meals are for any guest between 3 and preteen. Ask your catering company what options they have for kids and what is the cut-off age. Sometimes the kids can go through the buffet for half off the price. Other times the kids will get their own plated meals. Chicken strips are popular with all children.

There will always be guests with dietary restrictions. When you send out your invitations, just include a line that says, "dietary restrictions". Your catering team should be able to accommodate these needs. Make sure you document precisely who orders what and talk to the person in charge of your dinner numbers. This information won't be handed over to the catering staff until you are close to the reception. Find out when your "final numbers" are due. This will also help you with your invitation due dates. Give yourself an extra two weeks to collect RSVPs from your guests. A small list shouldn't be a problem. There always seems to be one guest who might not respond to you for some reason or another. It's important to ask your catering contact about your final numbers:

- After you give your final numbers, when is the last day you can still add guests?

Usually, when you give your final numbers, you cannot take any meals back. You will pay for the number you send in three to four weeks beforehand, even if the guests don't show. This is a challenging concept to understand, but if you look at it from the Chef's point of view, they are ordering and prepping all the food for a specific number of guests. Then you say the day of the reception someone can't make it. This is the fault of the guest, not the Chef. This is a big reason you pay for all the food before it's ever served.

43

This has more to do with larger weddings but will still be expected of small weddings and elopements.

For the reception, your options are wide open. There are so many to choose from: parks, halls, ballrooms, art galleries, hotel venues, cruises, wineries, barns, bed and breakfasts, museums, farms, beaches, yacht clubs, churches, estates, mountain resorts, historical buildings, ferry boats, conservatories, ranches, spas, canyons, gardens, castles, ski resorts, skyscrapers, restaurants, and family homes.

Before you sign a contract with a catering company, remember to ask the questions below. It's good to hear this early on and add this into the contract!

- What happens if you need to change the date?
- Or if you need to switch to delivery, can they accommodate changes because of Covid?

Wedding Tasting: Sometimes, when you book a catering company or a resort, they will offer a wedding tasting. It depends on the size of your group. Your wedding tasting will take place at their location, and you will be sampling all the food for your reception. This is different than most people imagine. You don't try the whole menu and narrow it down. You try the exact menu for your reception. This gives you an idea of how the entire event will look in one sitting. You are basically trying the food at a tasting to see if it needs more salt, less salt, more spice, etc. The Chef should give you everything you ask for, don't be shy in saying the salmon is a little under or overcooked for your taste. Usually, you don't give your direct feedback to the Chef because it will go through an event planner, a catering manager, or an email after you get home. In the end, we all must remember this is your event, and you know your guests better than anyone else. Rarely you will dislike a dish from an Executive Chef. They are trained at the highest level to provide elevated dishes. If for some reason you don't like a meal, it can be switched out. It's unlikely you'll be able to try a different item while at this tasting. Most banquet menu items are not on the regular menu and cannot be reproduced like a restaurant. There are usually a set number of items for the tasting. You can expect to pay more to try more items. Lastly, if you have a poor experience at the tasting or the food is not to the level you were expecting, re-think this vendor. If they can't produce the same exact food you will have at your reception during the tasting, it's hard to believe they can pull off a whole reception. Your guests will remember a great steak for the rest of their lives. I had to make this same choice three months before my wedding and changing to a different catering company was one of the best decisions we made. It went straight back to the undeniable awkward vibe we got at our tasting.

Décor, Linen & Lighting: These are all exciting to think about! They can make your day and night look magnificent. Once you have your venue and know what they offer, you can come up with a list of items you need to rent. A lot of the time, a wedding planning company will also have rentals. This makes the process easy for everyone. You tell them what you need and they bring it, set it up, and take it back with them. When you buy your own décor, different items will be going to other places: candles to dinner, the welcome sign to the entrance, etc. In my garage I had piles of the items going to specific places, and once we got close, I bought bins to match the size needed. When you purchase new items, make sure to cut tags or peel off the stickers before the setup. This can take five minutes at your house but can be very stressful if you left all of the unpacking for the setup day. Asking for as much setup time as possible will give your vendors enough time to stagger and not have too many people setting up at the same time. Buy the right batteries with some extras. If you have an idea of how you want the tables to be decorated, but you will not be the person setting up these tables, set it up at your house, take pictures, or use Pinterest.com to show the welcome or reception tables' ideas. Here's a list of items I've seen at weddings:

- **Arches** give you a backdrop for your ceremony and a place to stand. The arches are getting more and more creative with large circles and triangles. You can add flowers or silk. I don't recommend trying to make one yourself unless your husband happens to be a woodworker. These need to be set up by a professional, with stakes, so they stay in place and are secure.

- **Balloons** are used in all sorts of ways. You can put them on the road with directional signs towards your venue. The latest trend is balloon backdrop installations. These can look incredible and use all your colors. These can go on the arch, the entrance, or behind the sweetheart table.

- **Candles** are a soft lighting option that can make any room look elegant. Check with your venue guidelines before purchasing or renting candles. Some only allow flameless candles. They can line the entry to your ceremony, the aisle, the reception tables, the bar, mantels, windowsills, or basically anywhere that needs an accent.

- **Charger plates** are a larger fancy plate that goes under your dinner plate. They are very cheap to rent or buy. They can come in any color to accentuate your color scheme.

- **Ceremony and reception chairs** are not always the same, but they can be if needed. Your ceremony chairs will need to be set up by someone early on the day of the wedding, so other vendors can set up: florist, décor, and DJ. It's nice to have different chairs for the reception. If you don't, they will need to be moved by a team of people during the cocktail hour. That is no problem if it's only 20 chairs.

- **Lighting** has become so popular in the last few years. Bistro lights are the best way to illuminate an area without making it too bright. It adds an extra element of tasteful delight. If you happen to be doing the reception outside, it is good to turn on the lighting about 30 minutes before sunset. Twinkle string lights with battery packs are a good way to highlight areas that don't have outlets like a bar, railings, or mantles. Remember if you are outside to add lighting to bathroom areas, bars, the dance floor or stage, and walkways. Your vendors can share many other lighting options with you, especially if you plan on having a tent. It's good to keep your lighting company updated on your table layout and guest counts. They will be accounting for the extra space for tables being six feet apart. When you have lighting, you need power! This could mean you need a silent generator. Ask your lighting company how much power you will need.

- **Linen and napkins** are a must-have, and runners are nice to have. Banquet tables always need to be covered, but the linen wouldn't be necessary if you rented natural wood farm tables. There's a chance your venue will provide linen, but the colors will be minimal if they do. Elevated color choices will come at a higher cost. Shop around for prices before you confirm. Say your venue offers matching white napkins and linen. You could bring in colorful runners. If you rent these on your own, make sure you order extra: 2-3 linens and 10 extra napkins. When things spill, it's good to have a spare on hand.

❑ What are you thinking about your colors?

- **Silverware, glassware & dishware** can all be rented from the same source. The companies will allow you to pick them up the day before and bring back the day after, or they will simply deliver your order. You might need an appetizer, dinner, and dessert plate for each person. The glassware choices are water, wine, champagne, beer pint, and rocks glasses. Ordering one of each glass for everyone could be enough if your guests will use the same glass all night, but it's best to order a few extra just in case. The silverware will be a full set for dinner with possibly a steak knife. Don't forget the appetizer or dessert forks, if needed. Take note with Covid there could be particular requirements for handling and sanitation of dirty items. Check with your specific rental company for their suggestions.

- **Tables** you may or may not need: welcome table, sweetheart, farm, reception, bar, bistro, appetizer and dessert stations, cake, and unity table. See Chapter 6 for all of the table descriptions.

- **Tents** are good if you are worried about the weather. They can give shade from the sun and coverage if there's a chance of rain. Tents come in all sizes. Rental companies will set them up and take them down. Even though this is expensive, it is the only thing that can calm the nerves of someone worried about the forecast.

DJ & MC: This is the most popular choice for music. The DJ is a great way to go because they can help with your ceremony songs, cocktail and dinner music, specialty dances, dance parties, the microphones and speakers that go with each timeframe. They will bring a truckload of equipment, set everything up, and take it all down. The MC part can be very low-key for a wedding. They could ask your guests to be seated for dinner or announce the toasts. They help keep track of the timeline throughout the night. If you don't have song preferences, they can suggest something that has worked in the past.

Do you have songs you've dreamt about?

❑ Wedding party processional:

_____

❑ Bride entrance, down the aisle:

_____

❑ Bride & groom recessional:

❑ Bride & groom first dance:

❑ Father & daughter dance:

❑ Son & mother dance:

I do not recommend bringing your own speaker and having someone press play on a phone for the processional songs down the aisle. This is your big moment, and I have seen it go completely sideways when the technology doesn't work. This person could all of a sudden become very nervous. If we've learned anything about technology, there can be glitches when you need it the most! If you decide to do music on a phone for the dance party that can work all right, but it won't be amazing. If you do this, make sure you have charging cords, a speaker, and a playlist ready to go.

Florist: Decide what you want your flowers to look like. It's beneficial to share pictures of the specific type of flowers with the florist because they want your input to create your perfect bouquet. Ask the florist for their ideas about the local or seasonal flowers. Your florist might want to meet with you at your venue to walk through the different places you can put flowers, which could include: your arch, railings, signs, mantels, the aisle chairs, flower petals down the aisle, the welcome table, the bar, your reception tables, on the menu and cocktail tables. Some of these can be used twice, such as the welcome table and bar could have the same arrangement. Next comes your bouquet, your bridesmaids' bouquets, groomsmen boutonnieres, father and grandfather boutonnieres. Don't forget the mother and grandmother corsages, flower crowns for the bride or flower girls. These are only some of the things I've seen. The sky's the limit for flowers at your wedding. Anything you have seen in a magazine can be recreated!

Hair & Makeup: There are a lot of vendors that will do both hair and makeup. Some hair and makeup artists will travel to your location. Getting ready in a place where you feel comfortable and not traveling to different locations all day is fantastic, especially because of Covid. Either go to the website and choose hairstyles they already do or bring pictures of what you'd like to do. Most vendors will do a trial run on the hair and makeup. This is not required but is very helpful to make sure this is what you are looking for. This is an additional cost. On the day of the wedding, it will take a professional around 1.5 hours to do the bride's hair and makeup. It is nice to offer to pay for your bridesmaids to get their hair and makeup done as a gift to them. It's also good to extend the invitation to mothers, aunts, grandmothers, or any other ladies that will be getting ready with you. Regardless of who is paying for all the services, the artist will need a list of who will have which items done. They will also need a time as to when they need to be done by. The bride will go last, right before pictures. See the example schedule in Chapter 10. I don't recommend friends and family helping with hair and makeup unless they are in that industry. It can take double the time with an amateur and throw the entire schedule off. If you do rely on a friend, make sure to do timed trials.

Musician: Can be a harmonious way to welcome your guests to your wedding entrance and for the seating at the ceremony. I have seen a single violin, guitar, or a small quartet. These are also great for cocktail and dinner background music. They can do the processional and recessional songs for the ceremony. If you don't have specific songs, you can choose a particular music genre for them to play throughout. If vocals are needed, make sure they know that. Most of the time, the musicians won't help make any announcements unless you specifically asked them to say something. If you are considering a large band, this can be expensive. Bands are lively and can be a great party starter.

Officiant: This is the only vendor on this list that you need to be legally married. Some couples choose a family member instead of a professional. I only agree with this if they are, in some way, a professional speaker or your grandfather is a minister. When you don't choose someone who knows what they are doing, they will be nervous. This could take away from your ceremony. Things like reading incorrect lines, forgetting the rings, or looking red in the face will detract from the couple. If you go with a professional, they will meet with you before to get an idea of the ceremony. If you want them to be at your rehearsal walk-through, they can do that. If you were looking at a church ceremony you would have access to their minister but may require attending some meetings. Make sure you know what is included in the price of the church and the rental time frame. You will need at least three hours before to decorate and two hours after to remove the decorations. Decide who will be in charge of this décor. If you are doing an orthodox or catholic ceremony make sure you know the length of time it will take for your schedule. A few things to have in mind before talking to your officiant:

❑ Do you want any type of religion as a part of your ceremony?

❑ Do you want to keep it short or add a few things to make it a full 30 minutes?

❑ Do you have any action items planned during the ceremony like lighting candles, pouring wine, readings, songs, etc.?

Photographer: Photographers are there to capture your best moments. They will be able to take your wedding vision and put it in print. Checking out their websites is an excellent way to find your style and narrow down what you like best. You must meet with your photographer to match their charisma with your personality. Usually, the photographer will create a schedule for your day, and all the other vendors will work off that. Your schedule will be created from the time of sunset or the time of the ceremony. If you have a set time for your ceremony by the venue, the photographer will use it as a guide. Things to think about before you talk to your photographer:

❏ Will you do a first look? This is where the couple sees each other before the ceremony to take photos of their first glance. Some couples like to get all of the photography done to enjoy more of their night.

❏ How big is your family? You will need to provide a list of family shots before the day of the wedding. Check out the blog page on InsiderBride.com for a full list as an example. It can look like this:

- Bride, Groom, Jane, Jim
- Bride, Groom, all parents

❏ Where do you plan to do the majority of the photos?

❏ Will you be at the same location all day? Are there multiple locations?

❏ How much time will you need with the photographer? This will depend on when you want them to start and finish. If you want pictures during the getting ready and late-night dancing, this will be 10+ hours. If you want only basic photos of the ceremony, certificate signing, family/couple/wedding party, you could get that done in 5-8 hours, but that might feel rushed.

❏ Do you want any other items like a photo booth? Check out other items the photographer can do!

Transportation: Do you have multiple locations and not want a car to deal with? This is where transportation can come in handy. I took a town car to the ceremony site with my bridesmaids for pictures an hour before only three of us. Shuttles are a smart way to get your family and friends home safely. I've seen cute red trolley cars that have been turned into shuttles. There can be a round or two that takes people to their hotel at the end of the night. This all depends on the location of your ceremony, reception, and the hotel. A chic way to end the night is with a classic car driving away with the bride and groom.

"Love recognizes no barriers.
It jumps hurdles, leaps fences,
penetrates walls to arrive at its
destination full of hope."
- Dr. Maya Angelou

Videographer: This is the one thing most couples regret not having included in their ceremony. A video gives such a full-circle view of the special day. Seeing the ceremony later is so much nicer than relying on your memory alone. Your nerves could impede a recall of the ceremony or the rest of the day. A videographer can work closely with your photographer or even be on the same team. You can choose so many different styles of videos, whimsical, romantic, artsy, or even flashy. They will usually stay the same amount of time as the photographer unless you say otherwise. If you have special requests or styles, let them know with online examples. This is a good vendor to ask about a virtual ceremony; maybe they can help you live-stream the big day. Another new accommodation that has popped up with Covid is to send your guests a next-day ceremony viewing link. This is a way for your guests at home to watch the ceremony on their own time at home.

Wedding planner: There are two types of wedding planners: an outside and inside planner. An outside wedding planner or coordinator is a standalone event company that can help with everything. They will give you a list from full-service coordination to day-of coordination. The more you pay the more they will help you with. Full-service coordination has to do with all the logistics leading up to the wedding and managing the day. The Day-of Coordinator takes everything you have planned along the way and is only there to direct on the wedding day.

If you booked a venue, check to see if you have an internal wedding coordinator, planner, or event manager in charge of your wedding. They will help you plan some of your items, but not all of them. It is good to ask this person what exactly they will help you plan and their responsibilities are. As an inside planner, I oversaw the logistics at the venue and the timeline. I didn't do anything that had to do with decorations, flowers, music, pictures, videos, or something that a paid professional could do. Almost every couple asked me if they have me, why would they need an outside coordinator: I would say that if you want to relax and enjoy your day without lifting a finger, hire an outside coordinator. An outside planner will stop an inside planner from asking you or your family questions. Many things come up on the day that will need clarification. If you are the point person, you will get questions all day. The outside wedding planner can help with the following items and more: choosing and contracting other vendors, ideas about décor, set up and take down of décor or rental items. They will give guidance on your walking order, keep your schedule moving on time, have hard conversations with people who need them, and make the tough calls without involving you. They will make a disaster of a day come together seamlessly without you knowing anything. They are your go-to person from start to finish. My recommendation is not to involve a friend as your coordinator unless they have prior experience in event management. A friend will be even more worried they will mess up your big day, and I have seen this situation go south pretty quickly. Whatever you decide to do, don't go without a coordinator. Your whole event will suffer from a lack of direction without a professional planner.

This is what your vendor list should look like. It can be filled in as you confirm the vendors. The time of arrival will be the last thing you fill in once your schedule has been finalized.

What is one piece of advice for couples?
"Consider approaching your wedding like a styled shoot with the most luxurious food, desserts, rentals, and flowers possible for only your most favorite people. Treat yourself and those you love to an incredibly luxurious experience they will never forget. Focus on what you and your sweetheart dream of, and don't compromise." - Summer Robbins-Sutter, Owner of Summer Robbins Flowers

Company:	Name of Vendor:	Cell Phone #:	Time of arrival on day of ceremony:
Cake & Desserts			
DJ/MC			
Florist			
Hair			
Lighting			
Make-up			
Musicians			
Officiant			
Photographers			
Rentals			
Transportation			
Videographer			
Wedding Planner			
Other			

You will be confirming all the details with your vendors the month before. These will be final phone calls or emails. You'll make your full payments this month. Make envelopes with checks or cash ready to hand out for payments and tips at the event. It's customary to tip your vendors like you would a regular hairdresser. Check your contract to make sure the gratuity isn't already included. The chart below is a suggested guide to gratuity, which is always at your discretion. See HereComesTheGuide.com for more information on gratuity. If any professional goes above and beyond to fix a crucial situation, they would be considered for a higher percentage. I have seen couples write cute thank you notes and include cash or a gift card. Another way to let your vendors know how much you appreciate them is to give them a phenomenal online review. A few sites to choose from are TheKnot.com, WeddingWire.com, Google.com, FaceBook.com, or any other site you see a space for a review.

The Professionals:	Gratuity at your discretion:
Cake	$5-20/per set up staff
Catering	15-20% of the total F&B Minimum
Bartender	10-20% of the total bar bill
Décor	$5-20/per set up staff
DJ	$50-150 or 10-15% of the total bill
Dress	Is thoughtful, but not expected
Dress Seamstress	Is thoughtful, but not expected
Florist	$5-20/per set up staff
Hair	15-20% of the total bill
Makeup	15-20% of the total bill
Musicians	$15-25/per musician
Officiant	$50-$100 (depending on time spent with
Photographer	$50-200/each photographer
Transportation	15–20% of the total bill
Videographer	$50-200/each videographer
Wedding Planner	10-20% or up to $500

"Darkness cannot drive out darkness: only light can do that. Hate cannot drive out hate: only love can do that."
- Martin Luther King Jr.

Notes

Chapter Five

Let the real
planning begin!

Planning an wedding, especially your own, is a lot to undertake unless you have endless amounts of extra time. If you have a friend or family member who loves to plan events ask them for things that you might not want to do. Create a list of all the things that you are looking forward to organizing and then a list of anything in the not so much category:

Crazy excited about planning these items:

1. _____

2. _____

3. _____

4. _____

5. _____

6. _____

7. _____

8. _____

9. _____

Not too pumped about these tasks:

1. _____

2. _____

3. _____

4. _____

5. _____

6. _____

7. _____

8. _____

9. _____

10. _____

Things we already eliminated from our wedding:

1. _____

2. _____

3. _____

4. _____

5. _____

It might be useful to look at your lifestyle and how you approach tasks. Don't overwhelm yourself and try to do it all. Take one vendor at a time if that makes sense. Start a running to-do list, and everything you think of goes on there. Do not, under any circumstance, try to remember all the details because your mind will go into overload. By now, you should have a binder, spreadsheet, calendar, notebook, or whatever to keep yourself in order. This is not a time to start a new system. Look at how you already stay organized and keep it simple.

❑ Do you plan things on the weekends?

❑ Do you like doing a little each day?

❑ Do you have time at work?

❑ Is after work your only option?

Is there anything you are asking of the bride, groom, or family to do differently during Covid?
"I honor their comfort level. I have not yet worn a mask to actually officiate a wedding; however, 99% of these ceremonies have been outside, and it has been easy to be 6 feet apart from each other." - Wendy Duncan Owner of Wendy Duncan Ministries

I used a Google Sheet, and it went with me everywhere. This made it impossible to lose the information. If you want a copy of my template, go to the blog page on InsiderBride.com.

Planning in COVID-19 will be a full-time job. I recommend putting someone in charge of this from your group. This could also be an excellent task for a wedding planner since they are used to regulating strangers. There are many things to pay attention to before, during, and after your events:

- Having a list of every email and cell phone number for each guest attending.

- Keeping watch over the changing Covid guidelines in the state and county of the wedding.

- Your group might want to consider a quarantine before the big day

- Send out reminders to guests:
  - If guests are showing any symptoms to not attend.
  - If guests have been in contact with anyone with symptoms to not attend.
  - Communicating the necessary masks or items for guests to have while attending events.
  - Remind your guests of your Covid representative and their contact information in case they need to report a case after the event.
  - If a Covid case appears, that person will notify the guest and vendors immediately
  - Posting any required signs about hand washing and distancing.
  - Check that the venue guidelines are being met with sanitation stations in all required areas.

- Taking temperatures or administering hand sanitizer before entering the building.

- Make sure guests are following mandatory regulations such as wearing masks and staying 6-feet from each other during the event

- Be the contact person for any cancellations or switches in locations.

- Consider staggering arrivals and escorting guests straight to their assigned seats for the ceremony.

Please note that once you book your vendors it's not over. Each vendor will have a list of items for you to do. The DJ will want songs, and the florist will want your flower choices. After you sign each contract, you can ask for a list of items you will need to give them. This could be due in 9 months, but the sooner you accomplish these items, the better. If you know you're a procrastinator, then you need someone to help out. It could be your mom, best friend, or a wedding planner. Put the people in place to support your success. Finalize as much as you can along the way, so you're not left with a massive list at the end. The more you leave to the end, the more stressed you'll be the week of the wedding. The week before is when your family starts to arrive, and you should be enjoying yourself, not finishing projects. See a suggested timeline on the next page. This schedule gives you a year or more to complete your wedding planning. If you are on a shorter timeline, just pick the items you will still accomplish and do as much as you can daily. Three months is the absolute shortest time I would recommend to plan a wedding.

Suggested Timeline

Day of Wedding:
- Nothing! Your to-do list should be: wake up, have your favorite coffee or tea, go to the spa, get your hair and makeup done.
- Have checks written for payments, gratuity envelopes, or gifts ready to give out.
- The rest of the timeline will be the schedule with your vendors.

The day before your Wedding:
- Meet and greet new guests arriving in town.
- Bring in and set up decorations for the ceremony and reception areas.
- Do a rehearsal walk-through and rehearsal dinner.
- Give out any gifts to the wedding parties or families.
- Girls or guys night out! Are you sleeping in the same house as your soon to be spouse?

Two days before:
- Pickup any rental items or have them delivered to you.
- Get things organized and packed in cars.
- All bags packed: honeymoon, getting ready, and night of wedding.
- If you got your own napkins, this is a good day to fold them.
- Get your nails done.
- It's fun to do a small, casual dinner with anyone that is in town. This can be a good thing to hand over to your favorite aunt, parent, or anyone else that rented a house to host. Your only job should be to show up!

Three days before:
- This was the last day I worked before taking the rest of the week off. That's your call. You might want an entire week off.

A week before:
- Call or email all of your vendors and get the final schedule confirmed.
- Make sure all payments are taken care of, or the checks are written.
- Finalize your vows if you are writing them.
- Do final hair cutting, tanning, or waxing.

Three weeks out:
- Your final numbers are due for the reception, rehearsal, brunch, etc. Make sure you know the exact day they are due and that all your RSVPs are confirmed.
- Wedding presents will start to come in the mail. You can begin writing thank you cards. These should be completed a month or two after the wedding.
- Communicate with your guests. If you have an itinerary for the weekend, send it in an email and put it on your website. Example on the blog page.

Four weeks out:
- All of your DIY items should be done.
- All of your items should be purchased.
- All of your details with vendors should be wrapping up.
- You should be getting the last fitting for your dress.
- All your clothing and shoes should be ready to go.
- Marriage license, search your state requirements online.

Three months out:
- Your invitations go out.
- Figure out groom attire and all outfits for the bride.
- Order your rings.

Four to six months out:
- Finalize all your vendors.
- Confirm honeymoon plans and get visas if needed. With Covid maybe your honeymoon will take place the following year.

Seven to eleven months out:
- Shopping for a dress and bridal party dresses.
- Confirm the photographer and book an engagement session.
- Send out Save the Date cards.
- Create your wedding website and add a registry websites.

A year or more:
- Decide on your budget.
- Get organized and keep everything in one place.
- Book your venue for the ceremony and reception.
- Book a room block or rent houses, if needed.
- Register for gifts
- Start looking at all vendor websites.

What have you changed in your business to account for Covid?
"Masks, touch less temperature reading before each client, and call the day before to check on the health status of the bride and party. I need more time in-between clients to sterilize myself, makeup, tools, and chairs."
- Christine Colucci, Owner of Makeup Mafia

Notes

Notes

Chapter Six

Picking the
tables and chairs!

L et's dive deep into the fascinating world of tables and chairs. You must have your venue booked to read this chapter. Find out what your venue provides because every place is different. Be sure to get a list of what they offer. What is left for you to do? Outside wedding planners are invaluable with these details. They know the best rental places in town and all the pickup and drop off specifics.

Your ceremony seating during Covid will be different for each county in every state. Most likely, no one will be sitting in rows of ten. Check with your venue to see what the restrictions are for seating. If your venue doesn't provide a planner, this would be a perfect reason to have an outside wedding planner. They will have the most up to date Covid restrictions, as they change daily. Consider having everyone standing six-feet apart if it's a small wedding. Or in a church, you could mark off every other row. At the ceremony, everyone seats themselves, unless you have ushers. You could have programs passed out by ushers that mention the seating arrangements to keep everyone safe. You could do chairs in sets of 2, 3 or 4 with a six-foot distance and each family name on them. It can still look cute and be classy in this time of distancing.

As for seating at dinner, check with your venue to see if there are restrictions once you get closer to the date. Ask if the limitations are different for inside and outside seating. There could be mandatory masks, temperature checks, limited guest numbers inside, and no restrictions outside. Right now, you can do some pre-planning with the seating. On your guest list, start to group your guests that would be good to sit together. You could even ask this on your invitations, "Who are they comfortable sitting with outside of their household?" Some receptions have open seating where your guests can choose any seat at dinner. I have never recommended this choice. This was the one family fight I saw in my career. Family members were kicking each other off tables and telling people where to sit. All of your guests will want to sit as close to the bride and groom as possible, and if they are not told where to sit, they will start getting crazy. With Covid you might be forced into a seating chart. This is a good thing! You can connect like-minded people. Maybe your best friend from high school has never met your current best friend. That's a perfect seating match. For the reception, you might be restricted to seat only households together. Either way you can begin to group your RSVP'd guests together. If, for some reason, you get to do open seating, at the very least remember to reserve tables or seats for the bride, groom, parents, and immediate family.

A sweetheart table is a personal preference. Do you want to sit with your guests or at a separate table with your partner? I recommend a sweetheart table because you don't get too much time alone with your sweetie during the day. It might be the only 20 minutes you'll get alone. This may even help you eat something. The sweetheart table is also fun to decorate. Another option is to do a traditional head table. Where you sit with your wedding party and can include their significant others or not. This could be as small as four people or as large as 20. Again, it comes down to your group and what makes the most sense in combining people together. What about the kids? They can be seated at a kid's table or with their parents. This will depend on the age of the children. Be sure to ask the venue if they have high chairs or booster seats. If they don't, you can let the parents know, to bring their own items.

The reception tables are typically seated in ten or fewer guests, but Covid is changing that drastically. There are two choices for tables: round or rectangle. You can ask the venue the size of the tables available to you. Your florist will also want this information if you are doing any centerpieces. Round tables hold up to 10 guests on a 60" round, but that is elbow to elbow. It's better to seat 8 guests on 60" rounds. The rectangle tables come in two sizes, 6-foot and 8-foot. The 6-foot tables comfortably seat six, and the 8-foot seat eight guests. This way, you can always squeeze a person or two in, if needed. You could choose to have them longer by putting them together. You can also do a mix of round and long tables. Covid might force you to do small tables of 4 or less. For this you could use extra-large card tables at 38"x38". Anything smaller than 38" would be very tight for 4 guests.

Farm tables are high-quality long tables. These add a nice rustic look to the room. They will not need linen to cover them, but you will still need to add napkins or runners. They come in all sizes and can be rented. Check with your current rental company to see what they offer.

Rental chairs might match your farm tables better than the chairs at the venue. Make sure you see a picture of the chairs if they come with your site fee. Churches usually have metal folding chairs. These can be uncomfortable for more than 15 minutes. Chiavari chairs are the most popular rental because they come in any color you can imagine. There are wooden cross back chairs, which match the farm tables perfectly. With any rental chairs you can add seat cushions for an extra cost.

The ceremony typically has white or tan folding chairs. This is your call if you want to match the reception chairs with the ceremony chairs. The ceremony chairs don't need to be as comfortable as the reception chairs because your guest will only be there for 30 minutes. If you plan to have a longer ceremony than 30 minutes, start thinking about seat cushions.

Bistro tables are great for the cocktail area or displaying the cake. These are the tall tables that guests can stand around and mingle. These don't need chairs and hold about 4-5 people. For a wedding around 100 guests or less, ten bistros would be perfect because not everyone will use them. You can always go with one bistro table per ten guests unless you have extra space to fill. The size of linen to touch the ground on bistro tables is a 90" round. It does look nice to tie up the center with a ribbon in your color.

Oh, you thought you were done with tables? Nope! There's always more planning. Let's look at the rest of the room. You have a few more things to place: the dance floor, bar, dessert/cake table, entrance welcome table, and buffet (if needed). First, you can sketch out the reception room. Start with the entrance and get the welcome table as close to that as possible. Think about using furniture that is already available, like a side table. Next, look at the walls to see if there is a great backdrop you want for the bride and groom to sit in front of at dinner. Once you have that, place all of the tables on this side of the room. This will give you the opposite side of the room for the bar and the cocktail hour. Obviously, if this is outside, you can look at it the same way. Put the bar in a far corner with bistros in front. Do you need a dance floor? If so, it could be the same place that you had your cocktail bistros. If you have a food buffet, this should go as close to the kitchen as possible. But ask the venue where they usually have it located. They should be helping you with all of this planning since they know what works best. Lastly, the cake can be hidden until it's time to cut, or it can be on display. If you have other desserts coming, it's good to reserve a 6 or 8-foot table near the bar. This table could also be your appetizer station from earlier in the evening.

The bar will need some type of front. Rental companies have bars in all shapes and sizes. The back of the bar will need two 6-foot tables to organize the glassware and make a section for bartenders only. If you decide not to have a bar front, just use three 6-foot tables to create a u-shape. Order enough linen for these tables too. Rental companies also have full bar trailers you can rent. Think of an airstream trailer turned into a full serving bar. Your options are endless!

The appetizer and dessert table can be the same 6 or 8-foot table. Ask your catering team if they will need one or two tables for all your items. If you do not have an appetizer station, this table can still be multi-purposeful. You could place pictures of guests no longer with us as your memory table and then add desserts later. If you have a cake but no desserts, this table could be where your cake slices are collected after it's cut.

The unity table goes with the ceremony. It can be a place to set any of the action items. If you plan to pour a glass of wine or light a candle, this will need a table. It could easily be a bistro table that gets added back after the ceremony is over. Or you could bring something from home.

A welcome table is a place to greet your guests to your wedding because you will be hidden. I have seen flowers, engagement photos, a guest book, and a card box on this table. I have seen so many creative guest books lately; there was a globe, a pair of wooden skis, and Polaroid pictures hanging on a frame. You can add a welcome sign with your names next to this table.

❑ What will be on yours?

Notes

Chapter Seven

Everything else!

I know there is so much to think about already! Take your time and do things when you feel motivated, not when you're frustrated. The simpler you can make this, the better, always keep that in mind! So much that goes into detailing a wedding. Here's a list of questions to think about. Slowly start to answer them when you have time. Talk them over with your honey and see what you both like and dislike. Then when the specific vendor needs the info, you'll have it. You can, of course, change your mind at any point, but the more you make changes with the vendor, the more likely it will cause glitches later.

What is one piece of advice for couples?

"I know that this sounds simple, but my best advice is to just have fun on your wedding day and don't worry about what everyone will tell you "should" do. In fact, I recommend taking a few minutes after your ceremony, just the two of you (not even us or your photographers), and give yourselves a private moment to sink in that you just got married." - Stephanie Yun, Owner of Ace of Hearts Films

Here are all the random questions to go over with your wedding planner. Answer yes with your details, a no, or leave it blank if you are undecided:

Getting Ready:

❑ Where will the ladies and guys get ready:

_____

_____

❑ What type of food and drinks will the ladies have on the day of:

_____

_____

_____

❑ What type of food and drinks will the guys have on the day of:

_____

_____

_____

❑ Will you bring your own steamer for the veil and last-minute touch-ups:

_____

_____

_____

❑ Will you have your dress professionally steamed:

_____

$\mathscr{Setup}$:

❑ Who will be a part of your decorating team:

❑ Who will bring all the decorations in/out of the ceremony and reception:

❑ What is the setup time frame for the ceremony:

❑ What is the setup time frame for the reception:

❑ What is the overall concept for your décor:

Catering:

❑ What is your anticipated guest count for adults & kids:

❑ Are you having a post-wedding brunch? If so, where:

❑ Are you having a rehearsal dinner? If so, where:

❑ Will you have a plated meal, family-style or buffet:

❑ What food items are you thinking about:

❑ Will you need kid meals? If so, what types:

❑ Are there any dietary restrictions you know about (gluten-free, vegetarian, vegan, dairy-free):

❑ Are you interested in a coffee station:

❑ Are you having a cake cutting:

❑ Would you like the cake slices to be:
If you answered yes to cake cutting, circle all that apply below:
A) Passed to each person at each the table
B) To go back to a cake table
C) Save a slice for the one-year anniversary to go home with the couple
D) Save the top tier of the cake to go home with the couple

❑ Will you bringing special cake cutting utensils:

❑ Are you interested in late-night snacks? If so, what types:

Notes

Ceremony Venue:

❑ Will you have any pets in the ceremony:

❑ Will you need to borrow a unity table or anything additional for the ceremony:

❑ Will you bring in an arch or other large items:

Reception Venue:

❑ Will you need to borrow a welcome table or anything additional for the entry:

❑ What type of candles can you bring in: flameless, votives, hurricanes, or lanterns:

❑ Will you have assigned seating for the reception:

❑ Will you make the escort cards:

❑ Will you bring a sign to explain the seating arrangements:

❑ Are you having a sweetheart or a head table? If you have a head table, how many guests will be seated:

❑ Do you want round or rectangle tables:

❑ How many vendor meals will you have (usually there are meals for the photographer, videographer, DJ, outside event coordinator, and any assistants they have):

❑ Will you have favors or gifts to give out at the reception:

The Bar:

❑ Are you having a specialty drink:

❑ Would you like to offer a wine service at dinner or wine bottles on the table:

❑ Would you like to offer your guests a champagne toast:

❑ Will you bring your own special toasting glasses:

❑ What will be hosted vs. cash:

"There is never a time or place for true love. It happens accidentally, in a heartbeat, in a single flashing, throbbing moment."
- Sarah Dessen

The DJ or MC:

❑ Would you like to be formally announced:

If you answered yes, circle one below:

A) Announced to the cocktail area with your entire wedding party
B) Announced to the cocktail area without your entire wedding party
C) Announced to the dinner area with your entire wedding party
D) Announced to the dinner area without your entire wedding party
E) Other:

❑ How many people will be making a toast:

❑ For the toast:

If you answered yes, circle one below:

A) Would you like the toast once everyone has food in front of them?

B) Would you like the toast once everyone is finished eating?

C) Other:

❑ Are you doing specialty dances:

If you answered yes, circle all that apply:

A) Bride & Groom
B) Bride & Father
C) Groom & Mother
D) Other:

Extras:

❏ Are you interested in having other weekend activities available for your group? If so, what will those be:

_____

_____

❏ Will you be passing out gift bags to the hotel rooms:

_____

_____

❏ Are you interested in special transportation for you or your guests:

_____

_____

One of the last things you'll plan is your walking order for the ceremony. Many things will change from the beginning of your planning to the end. This is something that can change over time, so it makes sense to wait. You can start filling in the section below. This is one of the areas you can be creative. The officiant can walk as the first person to initiate settling the crowd in their seats. Or they can magically appear at the front and ask everyone to be seated. I've seen the officiant walk down the aisle alone or walk with the groom. Most of the time the groom will go down with his parents. The mother of the bride can walk with any important male in the family, like a son, brother, or uncle. Ushers can fill in anywhere on the list if someone needs a walking partner.

The traditional order is below, starting with the officiant. Do whatever works best for your group.

Officiant:

_____

Bride's Grandparents:

_____

Groom's Grandparents:

_____

Mother of the Bride and:

_____

Groom with Mother & Father:

_____

Bridesmaids & Groomsmen:

1) _____ & _____

2) _____ & _____

3) _____ & _____

4) Maid of Honor and Best Man: _____

Ring Bearer:

_____

Flower Girls:

_____

Bride & Father:

_____

The maid of honor is in charge of three items during the ceremony. They will fluff your dress once you are settled with the groom, take your bouquet, and remember to give the bouquet back at the end of the ceremony. The best man takes the lead on holding the rings. The last thing to know about the actual ceremony is for the wedding party to form a flying V from the couple. This works so well because it gives everyone a view of the bride and groom without having to lean over. It sounds like an easy thing to do, but when you have a rowdy group, they will be all over the place. If you have a wedding planner, they will go over all these items in the rehearsal walkthrough.

If you were to give one piece of wedding advice to the couple what would it be?
"Especially for this time, I would recommend couples to be flexible. Things are going to be different than expected, but if you can remain flexible and keep an open mind, it's possible to have an amazing event with your friends and family. We've put more focus into our micro weddings. Of course, we're still planning our larger weddings, but as things have shifted, we've seen more demand for smaller, more intimate weddings. And we love doing them! They are unique and fun, and we're able to do more stylistically with a smaller guest count. It gives us even more room to be creative!"
~ Bree Denman, Owner of The Indigo Bride

Notes

Chapter Eight

Your people!

Your family and friends will overstep in the planning phase because they don't know what's important to you. They don't know what a touchy subject is or not. They will want to tell you what they loved and hated about all the weddings they have ever been to. My best advice is to listen and thank them for their suggestions, then take them or leave them. This will be difficult to do, but in the end, this is your wedding not theirs. The hardest will be the parents. They always want what's best for you, but they might have outdated or outrageous ideas. They have been dreaming of this day for just about as long as you have, and they are an important part of your day. Most parents have an idea of what you should do, but that could be four opposite parental opinions. Usually, the person paying for the wedding has the most say, but not always. Everyone says this is the happiest time, but it is actually very stressful because two (or more) families are coming together. Tread lightly, my friend.

You and your partner will be going through many emotional stages: happy, freaked out, worried, excited, frustrated, overwhelmed, tired of waiting, and finally getting all of this over with. Be open and honest about your feelings since you could be in different stages at different times. Ask your partner what they are excited about, put them in charge of that. My husband wanted each part of the night to be a musical experience. He was in charge of 98% of the songs. That wasn't as important to me, so this was an excellent project for him. I've seen both a checked-out bride and a checked-out groom. Someone always seems to take the lead in planning because it comes easily to them. Go with the flow. Go with whatever works best for your relationship. You will remember forever that you got married during a pandemic, and that alone is an epic pursuit.

It's your decision to follow the traditions or skip them all. If you don't like cake, think about what you do like for dessert. Talk together, about which traditions you both want to keep, and if some don't matter to you, get rid of them. This is your wedding and making it your own style is crucial. Remember, you can always create new traditions. The very most important thing you can do for your own sanity is to keep it simple. If something isn't essential to you or anyone else involved, remove it.

As a Covid bride, you will experience more unknowns, because everything is unknown in our current world. We wake up on Groundhog Day again and again. How can you plan a wedding in such an uncertain world? It will be challenging, but you are a strong and capable human! You can do this! You will make the best of an insane situation. If you were on the fence about a decision, my advice would be to write down the question. Then post it somewhere you'll see throughout the day, maybe the bathroom mirror. Every time you see the question, answer it as fast as you can without thinking. This is a life hack to talk to your own intuition. It works! Whatever decisions you make will be right for you, even if that means holding off as long as you can to get through this experience in one piece. I believe in you! If you have followed your intuition, put the right people around you for support, and your partner is your rock, it will all work out. Stay strong and believe in yourself! My heart goes out to all the Covid brides taking on a pandemic wedding.

Here Comes Another One

How about the time I almost dropped the cake in front of the dining room full of guests? We had a wine room chilled to a perfect 55 degrees with a beautiful, copper top bistro table with a wooden base. Many brides would keep their cakes in there all day until it was time to cut the cake. On this night, we had a gorgeous three-tiered white cake with eucalyptus leaves around the base. Once everyone was seated for dinner, and before the speeches began, we would move the cake out for display. I asked a coworker to help me move the table. All we needed to do was clear a ¼ inch trim on the bottom of the doorframe. We went to lift the table, which was already heavy. Now it had an added 40-pound cake. We didn't clear the frame. In slow motion, the cake was falling towards my co-worker. I grabbed the bottom tier of the cake with both hands and held on for dear life. My co-worker caught the table and set it upright. It worked! The cake was saved! We tried again and made it to the final resting place. When I turned around to close the door, I noticed a table of guests who had seen the whole thing. I went over and said, "It's our little secret!" I rearranged the leaves to cover the two large handprints on either side of the cake. When the bride and groom came over to cut the cake, I had strategically placed the best side toward their cutting space. I told the couple this was their first puzzle to solve as a married couple. All they had to do is get enough cake for two bites onto a small plate. This was never as easy as it sounded, with a whole room watching in anticipation of a cake smash in the face. I hope someday that the guest table told the bride and groom the real story of the cake that almost didn't make it to the cutting.

"There is nothing I would not do for those who are really my friends. I have no notion of loving people by halves, it is not my nature." - Jane Austen

Notes

Chapter Nine

So many parties!

A ll the other parties are an enjoyable interlude on the way to the big day. Since we are in a time of Covid it's good to think about how each of these could be virtual parties. Many people won't travel, so it makes sense to look online for ways to make a party fun. Let's take a closer look at each one in more detail.

Bachelorette and Bachelor parties are typically done separately, but I've seen them as a joint vacation party in San Diego. The maid of honor and the best man usually take on the bulk of the planning to relieve the bride and groom. My maid of honor went over the top! She got a house in the city of my choice, with decorations, favor bags, dinner, fun games, presents, snacks, and drinks at the house with a night full of dancing. The number of things that can be done for a bachelorette party blew me away! Traditionally, you invite all the ladies within your age group that are invited to the wedding, with Covid that might not be the case. There are ways to be creative during this time, like go on a ladies' camping trip!

Bachelor parties can be wild, or they can be chill. It depends on the groom and his friends. Sometimes these parties never get planned until the weekend of the wedding. This can be the night before the wedding when everyone gets into town. But I've noticed a trend to have the night before the wedding to be a bit calmer, so everyone gets a good night's sleep for the big day.

Any woman you like on the bride's side can arrange the bridal shower. My mom did a fabulous job because she has a background in events. Our family tends to be widely dispersed, so we saved this event to be part of the wedding weekend. I liked the fact that all the women got to know each other before the wedding. If your group is much smaller, it could be done anytime leading up to the wedding weekend. Also, consider this could be done as a Zoom and have care packages sent to each house. Everyone can open their party pack together and play those games. There are so many new ideas happening in this strange Covid time!

The rehearsal dinner can be a welcome party for your weekend, and everyone's invited. Or it can be small and intimate. Customarily, a rehearsal dinner is only for the immediate families and the wedding party. It's normal for the groom's family to plan and pay for this event. This will completely depend on the style of the family and the venue you choose. Maybe you have booked a resort with multiple restaurants onsite. The rehearsal is easy to book with the venue and event planners that you already work with. It's good to know that most restaurants will charge a site fee to hold the room as a deposit. There could also be a food & beverage minimum on this event, depending on your party's size. See Chapter 2 for more about the F&B minimum and site fee. It sounds easy to host this at your house, but in the end, your home should be a place where you are hassle-free. Events are messy and have a lot of moving parts. To smoothly pull this off at a house, you will need the following supplies: food, beverages, flatware, plates, napkins, glasses, trashcans, music, enough tables, and chairs. Plus, it will need to be cleaned before and after the party. This is a lot to take on the night before your wedding.

There could be other events happening the week of the wedding. Some family members will fly in as early as a week before. If this is the case, it's nice to see the new groups of people as they come into town. You could designate a new person each day to host a brunch, lunch, pool day, hike, pizza party, or happy hour. Let it be totally their call, and all you have to do is let them know how many people you plan to invite. This would be something to go on your itinerary. If you want to take on these events yourself, I would recommend not having them at your house. You could invite the ladies to get their nails done or meet at your favorite coffee shop.

The post wedding brunch seems like just another big event to attend. Don't force yourself to do this if you don't like getting up early or know you'll be indisposed. Mine was at the hotel where we had our room block. We showed up 15 minutes late, everyone cheered when we walked in. It was pretty amusing. My favorite part was the Bloody Mary bar. You could also do a mimosa station with a variety of fruit and juices. Then we all said our goodbyes, and the weekend was over.

Are you heading straight to your honeymoon? This can add extra effort upfront but can pay off in the end. With Covid you could do a mini-moon and go off for a few days to a local place. This decision comes down to what your work schedules look like and how much time you can take off. If you are already taking a week off for your wedding, can you take another for the honeymoon? If you plan to travel to another country, will a week be enough time or are two weeks better? If you are going straight to your honeymoon, my only recommendation is to book it a day or two after the ceremony. This gives you enough time to decompress. I have seen couples miss their 5:00am flight the day after their wedding. This just doesn't make sense to rush and overexert yourselves. My husband and I saved ours for a few months later, which gave us something else to look forward to, and of course, Hawaii is incredible all the time.

❑ What do you have in store for your honeymoon?

Notes

Chapter Ten

Today is the big day!

It's now the day of your wedding! Make sure you have everything to make yourself happy from start to finish. Put all your favorite things in place for getting ready: coffee, breakfast, snacks all day, mimosas, or sparkling waters. It's imperative to eat during the day. Your adrenaline will be running, and it's easy to forget to eat. It's essential to eat before you start your hair and makeup. Take 30 minutes before you sit for hair and makeup to organize your items. This will be the last time you can gather everything before you're wearing a full dress. Hopefully, you have found a hair and makeup artist to come to your place. Once you are done with hair and makeup, it will take you 30 minutes to get into your dress, shoes, and jewelry. Make sure you build this time into the schedule. Once you leave for pictures, you will not return. Plan to have your bags pre-packed: night purse, overnight bag, and a bag that has extra makeup, water, easy to eat snacks, flip flops, sweater, phone, charger, etc.

Pictures can take 2-3 hours unless you don't want to see your hubby before the ceremony. You can still get a lot of photos done separately. The time depends on the number of photos and the number of people in these photoshoots. Most family photos are done during the cocktail hour. The entire schedule can be arranged for you to do the things you enjoy most. Maybe you like to dance and want a longer dance party, then move up the ceremony time. If you want to join your cocktail hour and see more of your guests, then do all your photos before. See the suggested timeline below.

The ceremony will be very quick, 15 minutes if you only do the basic lines. Otherwise, it will be 30 minutes if you have songs, speakers, or any action items. One tip I have is not to lock your knees. This can cause a person to faint. We don't want this to happen in the middle of your ceremony! Next, you'll go straight to photos. If you begin to talk to guests, you'll never get out of there. It's your wedding coordinator's job to take you to the staging area. Most couples go to sign their wedding certificate first. Your officiant and two witnesses are needed at the signing. It's usually the maid of honor and best man, but mothers would really enjoy this role if needed. Get your mom or friend to bustle your dress at this point in the day. Every dress is bustled differently. Pay very close attention to your seamstress when they tell you the way it works. At the very least, make sure it's bustled by the time you do your first dance. You can also remove your veil and put your bouquet back in a vase. After the pictures you get to rejoin the cocktail party or take a few minutes to relax, have a drink and a bite of appetizers. This is a sweet moment to take with your honey to see them before the rest of the evening takes over.

There are a few different ways to rejoin your party, either formally or otherwise. You can casually walk into the cocktail party and start talking to your guests. It's polite and expected to try to get across the room and say hi to everyone. This can be hard if you have big talkers. Do your best. If you decide to do a formal entrance at the cocktail hour, you wouldn't do it again before dinner. Sometimes it depends on the location and what has the best entrance location. Do you want to take your whole wedding party with you? This is totally your call, the wedding party will be expecting to do this, and if they don't, they probably won't mind that much. Your entrance can be just the two of you. The crowd will not notice either way. The only essential thing about dinner is to make sure you eat something. Everyone says this, because it's true! If you're planning on having even one drink, make sure there is something in your stomach. There might not be any other food coming your way the rest of the night. It must be said here that it's not a great idea to overindulge at your own reception. The main reason is that you won't have a clear memory of your wedding night for the rest of your life. If this is something you're worried about, elect someone to make sure you're eating and drinking water all night.

On to the speeches! This will take place around dinner. Some people have a dinner welcome speech or prayer. I would recommend not starting the speeches until everyone has food in front of them or gets through the buffet line. The standard speakers are the best man, maid of honor, one or both dads/moms, and the bride or groom. At the very least, one in the special couple should thank everyone for coming out of their way to be there. This could be a time that you include virtual well wishes from significant guests that couldn't attend. From this point, you can go straight into cake cutting or first dance. If you do the cake cutting first, it will give the cake cutters time to get it done while guests are watching you dance. The rest of the night can be dancing. If you want to throw the bouquet or find the garter, that's totally up to you! We made sure our DJ played our favorite dance song the first time she saw us both on the dance floor together. That was a fun memory that no one noticed but us! Late-night snacks are nice but a little over the top. No one is expecting any more food. If you decide to do some snacks, the best foods are sliders, pizza, or a nacho bar. The after-hours fan favorites are junk food. Sunset photos are nice, but not necessary. It will all depend if you have a setting that works for these photos.

"Gratitude is a powerful catalyst for happiness. It's the spark that lights a fire of joy in your soul."
- Amy Collette

Tentative Wedding Schedule:

9:00am – Bridesmaids' hair & makeup begin

11:00am – Bride packs bags and organize items for the rest of the night

11:30am – Bride starts hair & makeup

1:00pm – Get in the dress, shoes, and jewelry

1:30pm – First Look

2:00pm – Begin group photos for wedding party and family

3:30pm – Guests begin to arrive, hide the bride & groom

4:00pm – Ceremony

4:30pm – Cocktail hour until 5:30 PM

4:45pm – Sign the wedding certificate

5:00pm – Join cocktail hour, take a minute to yourselves or take photos

5:30pm – Seating for dinner

5:45pm – Bride & groom announced into the reception

6:00pm – Dinner is served

6:45pm – Speeches begin

7:00pm – Cake cutting

7:15pm – Specialty dances

7:30pm – All dancing begins

7:45pm – Sunset photos for Bride & Groom

The end - It depends on how long the venue allows or you want to stay

Notes

Notes

Chapter Eleven

It's over!

You did it! You're done unless you signed up to clean up your own party. I highly, highly recommend you pay the extra money to find a company to work on the cleanup duty. We found a company that took down all the décor, put it in boxes, and packed it in my car. Then put away all the tables, chairs, and swept. That was so nice to not have to deal with.

Some people go out to the bars after the big night. Most don't. It's such a long day you will be happy to just be sitting with your feet up. If you want to have the option to go out, book a hotel room in that area. Then you can meet up with people or not. It's a great idea to get a room the night of your wedding even if it's your town. This makes the entire day special.

You Guessed it, it's Storytime

What kind of wedding do you think I had?

We had around 100 guests. Our venue was in a nature reserve state park with a hall, patio, and bridge over a pond. My favorite part was that the wedding party would walk over the bridge to the ceremony. It was the reason we picked that venue. The only way to get to the other side of the pond was to use the bridge, or to take the path all the way around the pond. We started to hide the wedding party before the guests arrived in the aspen trees, which was just off the path. Most everyone was hidden by the time my

Dad and I walked slowly around the pond. I saw a few of my co-workers who came early and were already seated across the way. I had decided not to drink during the day, but when I saw someone had brought a glass of champagne over, I got thirsty! We got a waiter to deliver a tray of our passed champagne flutes to the group. Now we were having fun, and all my favorite people surrounded me! It still wasn't feeling real yet. Since I do this for a living, it was all business to my brain. When it was time to walk the aisle, I heard the song we decided on for our wedding party, "The Stable Song" by Gregory Alan Isakov. It was then that I began to tear up, and it was my turn to walk the walk. My mind was remembering all the brides I had sent down their aisle. My Dad and I slowly walked over the bridge to my song "Canon in D" by Johann Pachelbel. I was trying to make small talk with my Dad, but he looked very focused. I asked him later why, and he said, "He had an important delivery to make and couldn't possibly take a chance of messing anything up." We made it over the bridge, and I started seeing all the familiar faces that came to see us get hitched. I asked my tech-savvy cousin to stream the ceremony live because a few very important guests could not make the journey. Little did I know Covid was around the corner and this would become normal. The ceremony went smoothly except for the rings. My husband couldn't get my ring on my finger. I ended up looking out into the crowd with a funny face while forcing the ring on my finger myself. Our action item at the ceremony was a box of wine that we nailed shut. The box was engraved, and we both wrote a love note to open on our 5th anniversary. We decided we would write another note at our 5th anniversary and seal the box again for another 5 years. We casually joined our cocktail hour after the family photos. I wish I took more photos with the groups I talked to during that time. We had a buffet and the typical speeches. Instead of a cake, my new sister-in-law made her famous homemade pies. We danced the rest of the night away. The entire day seems like a dream. It went by so fast in just a blink of the eye. It came together flawlessly. Any hitch along the way is now just a funny story to look back on. I hope the same for you and yours!

"Love is an irresistible desire to
be irresistibly desired."
- Robert Frost

Notes

Notes

Acknowledgments

I am so grateful to get this out into the hands of those who need it the most and to be able to share my perspective on planning in a time of complete Covid madness. This workbook seemed to flow through me. The book's vision came to me at the beginning of September 2020, and by the middle of October, I had sent it out for the first round of edits. First, I would like to thank my husband, Devin Jensen, for designing the outstanding book cover. He has endured countless conversations about brides and weddings over the years. He sees humanity from a completely different perspective, which improves my overall comprehension of the world we get to be a part of today.

I would like to extend my sincere gratitude to my parents Lee and Marianne Jorgenson who worked on the editing and provided guidance along the way. Also, to those that were able to weigh in on important decisions and give infinite advice, my appreciation goes to my brother Jarett Jorgenson, my cousin Alana Reidy, my sister-in-law's Gitana Jensen and Tara Jensen. Also, to my friends Becca Whipkey, Elisha Herzog, Rissa Conway, Hillary Utley, Greg Fischer, Lara Brown, JoAnna Eisler, Kristi DiTullio, Sam Utley, and Stephen Conway.

My wedding knowledge comes from all the brides, grooms, mothers, and fathers who took this journey with me over the years. They are a part of my story throughout this workbook.

There is no way I could have done this alone. There was editing and then more editing. Special thanks go out to Ann Winfrey, Becca Whipkey, and Christina Aguet for all the corrections and adjustments.

Lastly, to the ones who walked the line with me every Saturday from May to October and on any other day. They have been there for every glitch the matrix threw at us. They saw me at my finest and on my worst days. There are infinite professional colleagues that held my hand along the way, so a thankful recognition goes to the ones who helped with this workbook: Benjamin Edwards, Bree Denman, Brittney Gamble, Caitlin Gallivan-Gaertner, Christine Colucci, Kimi Chassie, Marina Koslow-Davis, Stephanie Yun, Summer Robbins-Sutter, and Wendy Duncan.

"Being deeply loved by someone gives you strength, while loving someone deeply gives you courage."
- Lao Tzu

The Index

W

Y

Z

Made in the USA
Middletown, DE
15 April 2021